Through Crystalline Prisms

In Moments of Uncertainty

Angela Brownemiller

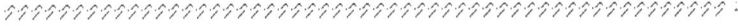

Through

Crystalline

Prisms

In Moments of Uncertainty

**KEYS TO
CONSCIOUSNESS AND SURVIVAL SERIES**
Volume 101

Angela Brownemiller

Metaterra® Publications

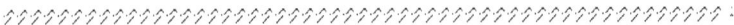

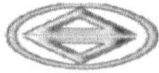

metaterra®
publications
THROUGH CRYSTALLINE PRISMS:
In Moments of Uncertainty

Copyright © 2020 Angela Brownemiller.
Copyright © 2012, 2020 Metaterra® Publications.

Published in the United States by Metaterra® Publications.
www.Metaterra.com
Library of Congress Cataloging-in-Publication Data.
Brownemiller, Angela.
Through Crystalline Prisms/Angela Brownemiller
1. Poetry. 2. Mind. 3. Brownemiller, Angela.
4. Consciousness. 5. Spirituality.
Title:
THROUGH CRYSTALLINE PRISMS:
In Moments of Uncertainty
ISBN 13: 978-1-937951-39-9
Published in the United States of America for US and
worldwide distribution.
Metaterra® Publications, USA.
Cover and content illustrations
by and copyright ©Angela Brownemiller.
Book design by and copyright ©Angela Brownemiller.
Ordering information and bulk ordering information available through:
Amazon Paperback and Amazon Kindle.
Also contact Info@Metaterra.com.

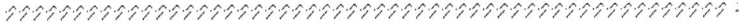

to the
precious
moments
of
uncertainty

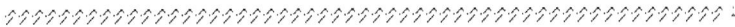

Through Crystalline Prisms

Table of Contents

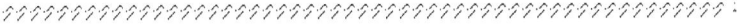

PART ONE

Crystal Missives

1.

Never Ending Stream

By what amazing grace
have we arrived here
lost and found
ending and beginning
again.

The thread
the spirit of life
weaves on and on
as we intertwine
with all around
and all within
and all eternity.

Never ending stream
all things
we were
we are
and
we will be . . .

2.
On the Other Side

Look

in the mirror.

Scratch

at the glass.

Can you

scrape away

the veneer

to see

your self

standing there.

Walk

into the space

other side

of the glass.

Transition?

Or return?

3.
Divine Imbalance

eager expression

rampant denial

of the confined

heart and eye

obtuse

mind floating

within body

idea within

disintegrating capsule

i see through

my forehead

grazing fields

of stars

nothing but

the flashes

are my own

dream of vapor

tremor of insatiety

the prolonged

the notion

that everything is bold

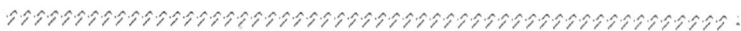

crushing and pensive

hostile yet waiting

forever to forget the

glowering of the sun

whose only desire is to set

imbalance of mere petals

stationed on the flower

stem asking only

for permission to

stand toward heavens

a tree is a hand

describing its own outline

against the sky

and living within

its own shadows

intermeshing

lightness and darkness

spasm of being

notion that all exists

at dawn:

the light

the sky

the dew in small webs

the washing stillness

the inevitable return to the seasons

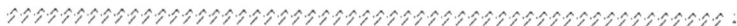

night and the dragon's eye
are hollow
a vacuum
sucking up light finally
like eyes of
a dead horse

beauty is in the impact
the stance
the second when
the heart
skips one beat
longing for relief
from truth
sucking day in
through the eyes

God
there is space
within me
for you
between the skins
of my cells
at the tops
of my breaths

i am the trembling vision
you call life

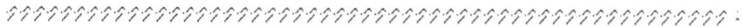

i am the flesh
of your soul
i am cartilage and bone
tendon and eye
muscle and liver
blood and skin

concrete highway
in a body
of carnage
passageway to
celestial glances

stubborn thoughts
of the holy
the elevated
the profound

one blink and
it all disappears
into the gaping mouth
of a ruthless infinity

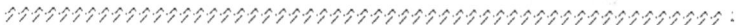

4.
Violining

Pulling the bow across the string
a tight wire waiting to sing.
The bow of old horsehair
wanting to share
something good:
the violin but a piece of wood.

Fingers play as fingers feel
pain and joy of sorrow and zeal
while music always always knows
worlds and tempos of joys and woes.

I am but the humble player
caught in the profound layer
of space between
what is known and what is seen:
music lives here.
This is clear.

Time may take me
life may break me.
But if I could be
more than I see
it would be music of my violin
singing like the rising wind

ʕʕʕ ·

in the endless span of starlit sky
and rushing tears rising in my eye.

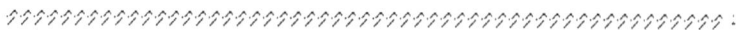

ʕʕʕ ·

5.
Eternal Journey

Wander on.
Realms, new realities
Having been here all along
Await.

Such a grand undertaking
Seeing this lifetime
Seeing this reality
As something the self can see as it wishes.

Such a step it is along the epic journey
The quintessential pilgrimage
The honoring of self.

Crystalline windows
Clearer than clear
Pure vision beyond all seeing.

Rush of sensation beyond
The material plane.

Consciousness Consciousness
Crystals of consciousness
Forming and unforming

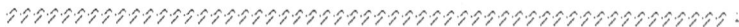

Becoming more than they are

More than they have known themselves to be

More than here and now.

Consciousness reaching beyond its fading limits

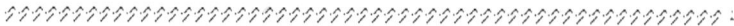

Because it can.

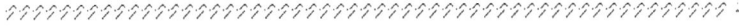

PART TWO

Fractured Populi

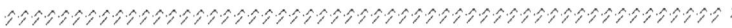

6.

Show of Hands

A show of hands
Cannot be wasted.

A true vote cannot be counted
Like a number.

Democracy cannot be bottled
Or injected.

The spirit of the people
Is massive and unseen.

Almost ubiquitous
If it listens to itself.

7.
Waving Mirrors

Each face a crystal soul
Trudging slowly up long paths
Pilgrimages to nowhere.

Eyes longing
The ground into walls
From earth.

Sands shifting mountains
Sadly eroding well into
More than nothing.

So much more than nothing it hurts.

Realization harms itself
Wanting no more than
Not to know
More.

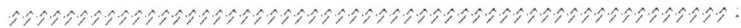

8.
All Too

All too true

These lies.

All too false

These truths.

All too solid

This vapor.

All too vaporous

This solid.

All too loud

This silence.

All too silent

This loudness.

All too

All

Too.

9.
Proxy Life

Proxy life
Lived instead
In place of.

Decoy truth
Spoken instead
In place of.

Substitute meaning
Understood instead
In place of.

Proxy reality
Is instead
In place of.

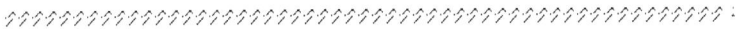

10.
The Crowd Called

Speech

The crowd called

Speech

Their hands clapped

Speech

Their eyes said

Speech

Their ears begged

For something ---

Something else

Something

Give me something.

Stop

Stop time

                Now

Stay

Stay here

                Where we can see

                You.

Don't go soundless

Away with your self

Where who you are

Is nothing.

PART THREE

Diminishing Apex

11.

I Can't Kill

Kill.

I can't

Kill.

I can't

Kill.

I can't

Do it.

Too weak

To make this work.

Too stupid

To see the way.

Too frozen

With ice hands.

One well knows

Moving through.

Still

I can't

kill

it.

12.
Moral High Ground

Opioid rhymes
Dangling fragments
Denying
Never realized dreams.

Altered truths
Staggering realities
Eternal missives
Waiting to be sung.

No message here
Seek no meaning now.

Walk away
Just walk away.

Take the high ground
Moral high ground
Immoral high ground
Plateauing at dishonesty.

Walk away
Just walk away.

Don't look back
You might see you.

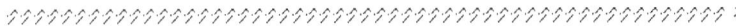

13.
Trading Later for Right Now

Rigid boundaries of truth fade
In the face of desire.
Trading later for right now
Trading meaning for sensation
Trading truth for illusion.

What longing inspires passion
What craving inspires longing
Sipping pheromone soup.

An unholy emptiness
A hole in time
A craven womb
Singing.

Love interrogating heart for truth.
Home is where my heart must be
The wild belong in the wood.

14.
A Kind of Eknosis

bear wolf

heart cries

silent signs

tears joy

desert rains

grounds break

rocks weep

stillnesses

thundering

underground rivers

gorging

living color

ravishing

winds

burial grounds

       burst alive

in the stillness

the heart cries

absolute joy

a momentary resurrection
its eternity apparent

sacred moments born
silent signs
savored....

such heart cries
light the way

thank
you
for this dance
with all
my heart

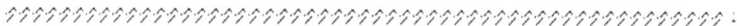

15.
Rushing

When nothing moves
Oceans stop.
Empty moments
Between waves.

You can touch the peace
The still a syrup.
Liquid reason
For nothing.

In that moment
Between crashing waves
I see
Where you live.

PART FOUR

Altered Erosion

16.

Show of Hands

In attempt to
Reenact the future
We collect ourselves
Old colored bottles
Congregating along
An older stone wall.

In the wind and storms
Some of us crack
Others are shattered
A few are left standing
Lonely and glossy
Seeing into the placid distance
Through bent glass.

Invisible birds loop through
These glass bodies
Intersection of wind and space
Yielding notes
Echoes of personalities born
Cast into the breeze
And the tendering
Of faces, faces, faces.

17.
We Have Been There

we have been there

old souls
in gowns and hoods
trudging slowly
up long paths
ancient narrow stone roads

we have wandered
longing for
satiety again

eerie and exotic rains
of foreign verses
ancient prayers in our eyes

touching of old mud walls
brings us home

for a moment
fleeting sense of gravitation
through time
through chaos and lights
of this universe

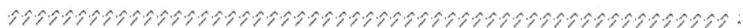

through our minds
thick with flesh
heavy with these bodies

to our hearts
our homes
our hands

wizened
spirits

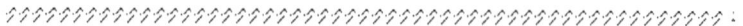

18.
Waiting for Centuries

early star houses

waiting for centuries

their windows

deep and vacant eyes

empty with the presence

of the universe

empty with the meaning of life

time and civilization

empty of the earth

which reaches up

from the ground

composing itself

from the ground

into walls and shelters

capturing spaces

making them dwellings

dwellings of the soul

the seeds of time

have confronted us

posturing

another form of existence

another aesthetic

another stairway to the stars

everywhere

everything formed like star houses

of the earth

and eroding back

into the earth

freeing spaces

freeing these old hooded souls

trudging

up stardust pathways

in search of everything

they already see and know

nothing is ever lost

ever

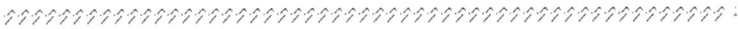

19.
The Memory

If the history of the world were a night
we would perch now on a hill
overlooking an encampment
the flickering of lanterns
in the wind
the passion in the passing
of time....

If the history of the world were a night
we would be children
on our bellies in the mud
spying down onto the village
out over the sea
stars flickering in the sky
mirroring our glances
lights on earth....

If the history of the planet were a sea
time would be a lady pirate
riding on celestial wind
eyes into the sky
arriving on our hill wearing
red silks, blue sashes, black capes
teeth round her neck

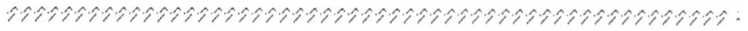

rings in her ear....

If the history of the planet were a sea
the children would swim to
the water ship for stories
water would show them the night sky
ridden with robbers and gods
and take them to a hill
overlooking an encampment
and watch with them
suspense in their fire lit faces
the flickering of lanterns in the wind
and the passion in the passing of time.

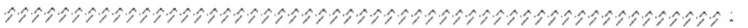

20.
We Forget

How soon we forget
as the land forgets its particular
nature at sea and rolls inward
as the babe forgets its chubby flesh
and grows rigid and aged
as the scar forgets its wound to heal.

As the iguana has forgotten
the spiral life of the slug
the wasp has lost
the sea from the crab
the flower forgotten by
the wings of the butterfly
or the bird who thinks
she has never been an angel.

Ah, the scholars denying dragons!
a night who does not know
the path traced by a hot red sun.

How soon the legs forget their bodies
the fingers their hands
the lungs their veins
the senses their souls.

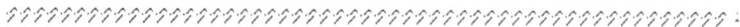

Archaic crustaceans
etruscans in sanded rocky pools
forming out of the sea
screaming with eyes
and water and flesh
boiling with the inventiveness of life.

Spirited horse of evolution
benevolent monster
octopus through time.

How soon we forget the galaxies
and the light years traversed to be here
to encounter these faces in the sand
our own reflections in silvered mirrors.

Ideas forming countless visions into bodies
vast detailed populations
organisms all on the march.

How soon we forget
our venous presence
through life and time.

So rapidly
that which
our eyes have seen
is faded.

How soon we forget.

Yet

how strong is the memory.

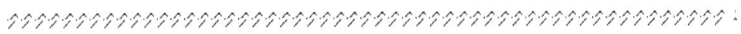

21.
Perched on the Edge

Perched on the very edge of life
teetering between worlds
someone is giving out
licenses to switch beings.

In the crystal distance we glimpse
ironclad knights on white horses
galloping down long turquoise beaches
and those women dressing in crepe gowns
parading on air in long lines.

We are gathered here today
under the chartreuse trees of reflection
an airy vision, an empty day
brimming with its own subtle volume.

Is that the future looming
like soft dusk over the horizon
the sunset a battle between worlds
at the door to the white forest of stars?

We seek to resolve
the agonizing imbalance
of an incomplete circle
reminded that weightlessness

is a reasonable experience
in outer space.

Now we are swimming like land
to reach sea waters at shoreline
cupping our hands to fill them with sky
and feeding our souls
through the door of our eye.

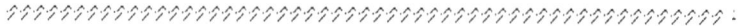

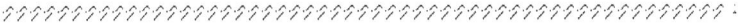

PART FIVE

Vanishing Drama

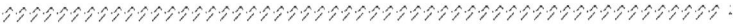

22.
Skies

Philo skies

Itching with blue

Daily different

Ever transforming

Motion the constant.

I stop

I stretch

I reach for the sky

Elusive illusion

Close down

Dark grey

Rabbits foot here

Rabbits foot there

Stampede of sheep at bedtime.

Old lace

Spiders

Rhythms

Shot like an idea on the horizon

Rocketed through time

Ode, an ode to ever present motion.

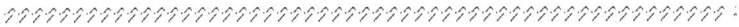

23.
Trying to Tie

Moments end

When

Trying to tie time

To markers in the

Space of nothing

Markers in space unhinged

Markers in vacuums

Sucking what is

In

Trying to tie

What is to what is not

What is real

To itself

When it is not really

Real.

24.
Just

just my daddy's dream

things are not as they seem

in the land of do's and don'ts

there is a small room for a child's won'ts

but they grow mute in the face of pressure

her force of will grows lesser and lesser

daddy's dead now

lives in the sea

recycled

his ashes fly

what is

a funeral without a permit.

25.
Bleed and Sing

Out of the storm
You stumble up the hill
Your ravaged soul so worn
Saying you're here by sheer will

You walk in the door
Pleading for mercy
Almost fall to the floor
Then you say purely

You say,

I'm hungry
So feed me
I walked all this way
But just let me be
I'm not here to stay

I'm not here to change
I'm not here to pray
I'm not here to rearrange
I'll soon go my way

I'll play for my food
I'll sing you a song
You give me some fuel

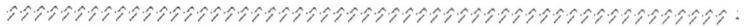

This can't be wrong

So you drag to the piano
You sit down and play
And as best as I know
The rest goes this way:

You like to bleed and sing
You like to bleed and sing
You like to bleed and sing
You like to bleed and sing
You rip open your soul
Get down with truths
And then rock, oh and roll
And then sing the blues

Oh how you like to bleed and sing

You think there's something in the bottle
The spirit o' the blues
It sparks your throttle
So you can really sing the news

So you
Chip away at your edges
Erode to the bone, gut and heart
The ol' booze you think that's what dredges
Up the guts of your art

Oh how you like to bleed and sing
Yes bleed and sing

You're not here to change
Not here to pray
Not here to rearrange
Not here to stay

Oh you walk on earth
A stranger, a god
Hinging your own worth
On a gut wrenching odd

You do like to bleed and sing

26.
Fly with the Phoenix

You can
make a comeback.
It is never too late.

You find yourself
struggling
in the rubble
of broken dreams.
You have been there
a moment, a month, a decade –
however long.

You may feel your pain
your tears
your sense of loss
your hopelessness
or you may just feel
confusion
or you may just feel
nothing at all.

You say please
please someone
fix this.

Please please
show me a way out.
Please please
God, if you are out there
help me.

Bits and pieces of
the life you wanted to lead
lie around you
shattered.

You may weep
or you may scream
or you may sit
in numb silence.

You tread carefully
through the fragments
of your fractured dreams
because you hurt
when you walk on them
as if they are broken glass
and your feet are bare.

Everywhere you see
wasteland
your own personal wasteland.

But these bits are the

ingredients

of something new.

Put them together

like pieces of

a jigsaw puzzle

and you will solve

the mystery

of the new you.

There is a secret there

among those ruins

there is something new

waiting for you to see.

There is always

time to begin again.

A hand reaches

out from somewhere

a hand you can almost see.

Is it your imagination

or is there someone there?

Look again

the hand you see is your own.

Yes there may be others

trying to help.
Or you may be
all alone in this.
But the hand you see
is your own.

You are calling yourself
back to life.
Listen.
You want to be
heard.
You want to
come back.

The view from this
rock bottom place
is the most profound view ever.
Open your eyes.
From here you can
truly see.
The possibilities of
consciousness are endless.

Believe that you can
resurrect yourself
whatever self is.

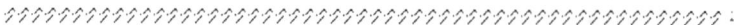

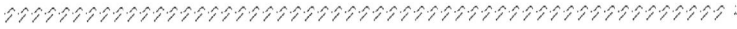

Believe

and you will carry

who you truly are,

your spirit,

on.

See you on the other side.

27.
Seven Times Broken

cold hand

broken now

slippery eye

lost face

curved mind

trapped word

blue dry flesh

there is an art

to being

sheer existence

involves

being sentient

of something

or does it

ideas

shake themselves

empty

of depth

dust

of substance

chasing itself

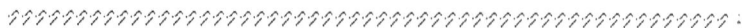

soaring blind

on broken wing

in winds of eons

of sensation

of thought

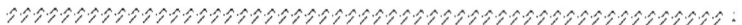

PART SIX

Deluded Love

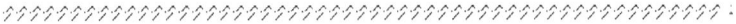

28.
Over and Over

if i could put
my light
into a ball of love
and give it wings
it would fly to you
and fill your heart
rushing into you softly
until your blood sings

if i could be
an angel on high
i would fly to you
over and over
kissing the air around you
stroking the space within you
loving the pulse of your heart
your life force my light

when i would become you
and you would become me
and we would become one
i would know
because the sky would rain
stars from the heavens

like water falling to earth
and becoming its seas

rushing into ourselves
oceans of us
dissolving

29.
Where You Left It

now cartoon land is back
where you left it

inside here
in this mirror world
solids evaporate
to the touch

longings dissolve
for no reason

empty feels good

                    cry
a tear at a time
then go

30.
Knowing You Cannot Find Me

knowing you cannot find me
in the dark of my night
you cannot catch me
when i run so wild
you cannot hold me
when i am sometimes nothing

you once told me
never stop on bridges
it still brings tears to my eyes
to see we have reached
an impermeable impasse
overture to time

i try to burn
pictures i have of you
i cannot
but this railroad
rides one way
not home to you
or me

31.
Last Call

I am a woman alone in a dream
with a man who cannot see me.
I can fashion myself
from mistress to monster
in his eyes.
I can lay waiting for his love
thrust in the dark.
I can plan to close my heart to him
doubting he will feel.
Doubting he will feel regrets
a flower mistaken for a thorn.

Wiser now
leaning on time for support.
No words no screams to explain
what time has buried.
History lies history deceives.
What we were we were not we are not.

Alone on the path of us
I see the girl you hurt.
Alone on a path you never walked
alone on a way you never wandered.
She sees you were never there

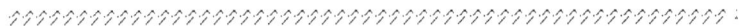

you were never hers
you were never.

You fade
into the distance
receding horizon speeding into nothing.

Wait
come back to me
you who never were to me who never was.

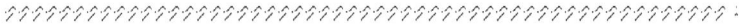

32.
Years

Through the years of desperation
We have arrived here
To know the humility of love
And the layers of being

The turmoil of time and change
Cannot separate us now
Nor bring us together
Again
If ever

Friends is cheap
Lovers is lying
Acquaintances is not the case

Clasp and consider
A flower in spring
Bursting with itself
Or an enormously
Soft cat
Watching
The day follow itself with a new dawn

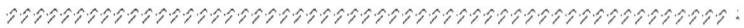

Why not
The feel of skin in the night
Unfolding into a new prison

Broken streams glowing
Shattering
For no reason

There really is
No way home

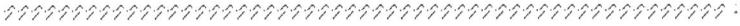

PART SEVEN

Women Screaming

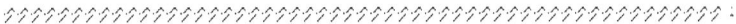

33.
Perfect

Women with no arms
Walking on tightropes
Ending in mid air.

Dead end
Once worshipped
For its meaning.

No exit
No turning back
No way out
No way in.

Iotas of meaning
Seep from their eyes
Like dry tears
Doubting even themselves.

Aspiring to heights
Grasping to reach
For nothing.

34.
Imperfect

Like women
dressing
in crepe gowns
parading
on air
in long lines.

I am
your willing captive
prisoner
of need
no exit
seen.

Imperfect
flawed
not whole.

But
I am indeed one
I am one with nothing.

35.
Plastic Now

out of the weeping mouths
of aging babes
their breasts are plastic now
cheap change

vapid solemnity
wanna be hoars
hands out saying
give me love

they will pay some way
buying shells
of selves
to wear

sex irrelevant
face of growing older
older without a man
as if he could bring identity

tramps fear
of growing older
without a self

no throw away self
once discarded

36.
Tree of Tears

Mossy
Tree of tears
Weeping soft fronds

Slipping breezes unfurling
Longing wands growing down
Into deeply unseen wilts

Hearts of newer life
Eye keys pulse
Dreaming

Green now

Quiet still crashing
Downing falling forest
Of but one lonely tree

Roots unearthed
Blown away
Whisper.

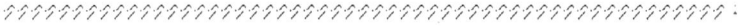

PART EIGHT

Core Emerging

37.
Riddle for The New Year

Yet another year

has made its way

into

the storage shed of time.

There amidst the bicycles

bags and bundles

is a pile of papers

held together

with a piece

of pink yarn

and a

glossy maroon datebook

with the numbers 2008

or some year like that

in gold

on its cover.

All dressed up

with nowhere to go

anymore

its job is done.

Now this datebook

looks forlorn

out of place

because it hasn't yet collected

enough dust

to blend in

with its mellowed surroundings.

Time, time

good good time

where do you go?

A tinny sounding radio

is offering

the question of the ages

its inquiring music

wafting over

from the neighbor's house.

O.K., so time

where did you go?

The datebook falls open.

May something, dentist.

September twelfth

dinner at Dan and Ann's.

Out of town

here and there all year.

Meeting lunch.

Meeting at the school.

Meeting at three.

Meeting on Saturday.

Check-up.

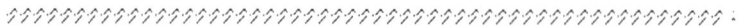

Auto maintenance.

Meeting Tuesday four.

Shots for the dog.

Child care.

Meeting. Meeting. Meeting.

All the little and big

appointments

seem to

make the world go round

or at least

make your head spin.

Tempus Fugit.

Sure, time flies.

You can't catch it.

You can't save it.

It doesn't come back.

But memories do.

They arrive

like anonymous letters

and packages

on the doorstep

of your mind.

Some are gifts.

Some are packages

you'd just as well

not open.
But they
arrive anyway.
Little pieces
of yesterday.

With time
2008 will leave fewer
of these parcels for you
but there will
always be some
coming back to you.
A little like
self-addressed
stamped envelopes.

The wind begins
to blow insistently
in through
the open shed door.
The datebook
blows closed.
Papers
and other loose items
ruffle
in an orchestration of days
months and years past.

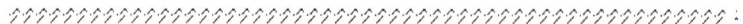

Something is calling
your name.
You feel its hands
tugging at
your heart.
A longing fills
your chest.

The neighbor's radio
begins to blare
Peter, Paul, and Mary
my bags packed
ready to go
standin' here
outside your door
babe I hate to go.

You feel for a moment
you miss 2008
like a lost lover.
Your heart
cringes at the sight
of the maroon datebook.

Nostalgia hits.
Teary eyed

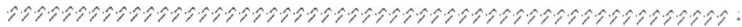

you sit on a limp carton.
Will it hold your weight?
It collapses only a little.
You spot an old Kleenex box
leaning out for love and
trying to be useful.
Good.
You cry a little.
You laugh a little.
You punch
a few stacks of newspapers
very hard
just to see how it feels.
You throw the poor datebook
at the wall.
You get those feelings out
saying a rich adios
to an entire year of your life.

Then you start to feel
a little bit differently.
There is room for something new
like this year for starters.
You breathe freely
for a moment.

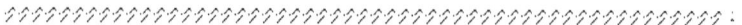

Suddenly

a cat lands on the cold tin roof.

You awake

out of your reverie with a start.

When you stand up

your hands feverishly

wipe away the dust and cob webs

from your soiled pant legs.

A few memories

are torn off

like desperate bugs

caught in the flying webs.

You look around aghast

realizing

you are in YOUR NEIGHBOR'S SHED.

You leave

anxiously closing

the rickety door

tightly behind you

hoping that the memories

can't escape.

As you sneak back

into your own yard

you are happy

you don't have a shed.

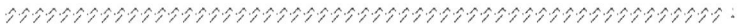

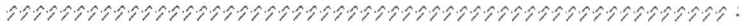

What would YOU have stored there?

What song is playing

on YOUR radio right now?

Where are YOUR memories kept?

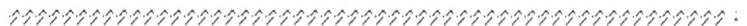

38.
There Was a Note

There was a note
resonant and solo
played once long ago.

I heard that note
through the fog
of my pain.

It came into my ears
like light
in the dark.

I followed the note
along a path
to more sound.

I heard the sound
as many notes
through time.

It came to me
that this was a
concert.

I followed the stream
of music to its crescendo
and found myself there.

I thought I had been lost
until that moment
of truth.

I thank God for music
as it has saved me
from a dead life.

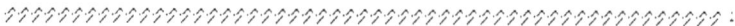

39.
Savor the Moment

Savor the moment
the story of this
moment.

This is
after all
your moment.

No word will ever
capture the taste
of this time
the wash of this
ecstacy
coming over you.

In this moment
the wine of now
touches you.

Know this moment
know this wine.

The finest things
are hard to get.

Go to them now....

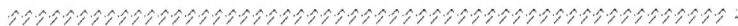

40.
The Great Unfolding

By what truth

do we see

truth.

By what eye

do we see

time passing.

By what touch

do we see

walls dissolving

into space

and time beyond.

By what thread

is woven

all we know

and

all we do not know

we know.

We are the

never ending stream

of all things

transforming through

life and time

to be in their own

life and time.

41.
On This Plane

We are but sight seers

On this plane

On this planet

Til our visas expire

Pieces of a mosaic

Hurtling forward in time

To become a whole picture.

Take off your coat

Kick off your shoes

Stay awhile

Rest in peace

And then go back out for more.

42.
Next Step

There is always

A next step

Just past the end

Just beyond the place of no exit.

There is always

Hope.

Realms, new realities

Having been here all along

Await.

Such a grand undertaking

The epic journey

Calls.

Capsules of truth

Wisdom finding its way

Into our knowings.

Now time comes together

Like all roads

Leading to the same place

Pressing the knowing

Into sight.

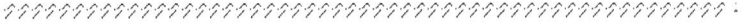

PART NINE

Intention

of an

Ailing Species

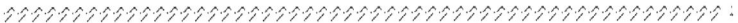

43.

Fortress of Intention

Fortress of intention
Armed with meaning
Of some sort.
Yet a holding pattern
Is not in itself
Peace.
Or is it.

Foes greeting silently
Nodding agreed
Not to harm.
Each other or themselves?

Walls have seen transgression
And promise
And war.

Walls have seen walls.
Boundaries of intention
Separation of purposes
Borders can be clashes.
Identities divided.
Identities of people.

Being people is not being

Designated as anything.

Or is it.

Can you wish peace into being

Or perhaps instill it in people?

Can you take the boundary out of an idea?

44.
Paradoxical Denial

Hurtling toward extinction

Too willing a demise

Breakdown of wholes

Schisms of collective mind.

Crack in structure of species psyche

Furtively unlearning

Decrying population wisdoms

Unknowing that "me first" kills.

Survival of the fittest quietly reveals its myth

When the good of one is not the good of many.

Are we in line for a dose of our own medicine?

Table that thought

Ignorance is bliss

Too much truth hurts

Fear is pain

Reality is shock.

Denial is the preferred mechanism

Of the human species facing extinction

Paradoxical group denial

The salve

Yet itself the very killer.

45.
Precious Moment
Of Uncertainty

Ultimately

spartan illusions propel us

racing ahead to clear the way

for untruths

for lies

for realities we want to believe in

for wanton elixirs

marathon of preferences

fabrication of ideals

consumption of stock and trade

belief systems…

To trade the charade we are living

for something else

an awkward undressing of us before us

on the stage of us

stripping ourselves of us

for what?

for what we posit we know…

Can we pray something into being

manifest something into recognition

wallowing in

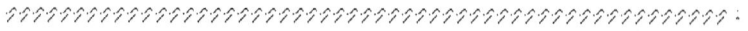

this precious moment of uncertainty

which is perhaps the greatest gift

a moment of synaptic elation

surfacing from pure unfiltered confusion…

This is where

the answers are for us…

a species sleeping

on the edge of extinction.

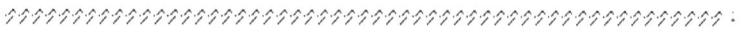

Dimensions and Refractions:
Afterword

Through Crystalline Prisms wishes to lead the reader on a little journey of immense and minor proportions. Piece by piece, poem by poem, step by step, these words invite us on a pilgrimage into our own hearts and minds, our own selves. Fragments of knowing ripple into sight. Little phrases crack open realities, like keys to places we did not know we could access. When we reach our selves, we dissolve into more than we are. Finally there, we ask where...who...what. Yet there are no questions, not really. There are only infinite spaces full of essences framed by these lines, these crystals we say are merely poems.

We seek the side effect of reading through. Visions, sightings of dimensions of reality we may not ordinarily see, are captured on these pages. Like birds being set free, these words fly out into the ether, shift form, and touch us. Presences and realities are summoned, veils are lifted, and between the lines we see dimensions of the here and now, and of the beyond. These are dimensions we have a right to know, to travel, to calculate into our minds and souls: into our lifetimes, moment by moment.

Poetry indeed designs keys that can unlock places we may not know are there to visit. Poetry also unlocks places we may be otherwise prevented from knowing exist. These lines refract light into truth, the poem being the crystalline prism shedding light on all that is, was, will be.

Angela Brownemiller

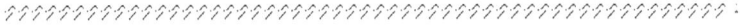

Metaterra® Publications

**Readers, walk with us,
share in the harvest of
culture and mind,
spirit and soul,
idea and letter,
history and the time it travels....**

Metaterra® Publications seeks to bring together modern and ancient issues and ideas.

Metaterra® seeks to harvest the matrix of intellects and wisdoms, to develop new and build on existing and old approaches and philosophies.

On the Metaterra® book list, you will find both nonfiction and fiction, and some of what lies between, and some of what lies outside these parameters. Consider this Metaterra® Central here and beyond.

www.Metaterra.com

Among the Books by this Author,
Dr. Angela Brownemiller,
are other volumes in this ...

**KEYS TO
CONSCIOUSNESS AND SURVIVAL SERIES:**

Poetry and Consciousness:
Volume 101: **THROUGH CRYSTALLINE PRISMS**
Volume 102: **IN SILENT RUSH**

Consciousness, Survival, and Psychology:
Volume 3: **UNVEILING THE HIDDEN INSTINCT**
Volume 4: **HOW TO DIE AND SURVIVE**
Volume 5: **OVERRIDING THE EXTINCTION SCENARIO**
Volume 8: **NAVIGATING LIFE'S STUFF**

See also these books by this author:

SEEING THE HIDDEN FACE OF ADDICTION

THE POLITICS OF PERCEPTION

Additional works by this author are listed on:

Amazon.com
and
DrAngela.com

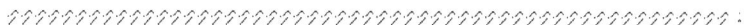

About the Author

Internationally recognized author, speaker, trainer, clinician, psychotherapist, journalist, guide, Dr. Angela Brownemiller, also known as Dr. Angela®, is author of numerous books on the human mind, consciousness, and sprit, as well as several books of poetry. Among Dr. Angela's works include the *KEYS TO CONSCIOUSNESS AND SURVIVAL SERIES.*

See DrAngela.com and Amazon.com
for more information and a full booklist.

Author contact:
DrAngela@DrAngela.com

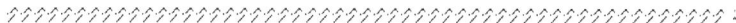

www.ingramcontent.com/pod-product-compliance
Lightning Source LLC
Chambersburg PA
CBHW071227090426
42736CB00014B/2995